Don't Drop the Mic— Study Guide

The Power of Your Words Can Change the World

BISHOP T. D. JAKES

Faith Words

New York   Nashville

FaithWords
Hachette Book Group
1290 Avenue of the Americas, New York, NY 10104
faithwords.com
twitter.com/faithwords

First edition: April 2021

FaithWords is a division of Hachette Book Group, Inc. The FaithWords name and logo are trademarks of Hachette Book Group, Inc.

The publisher is not responsible for websites (or their content) that are not owned by the publisher.

The Hachette Speakers Bureau provides a wide range of authors for speaking events. To find out more, go to www.hachettespeakersbureau.com or call (866) 376-6591.

Library of Congress Cataloging-in-Publication Data has been applied for.

ISBN: 978-1-5460-2946-5 (trade paperback)

Printed in the United States of America

LSC-C

Printing 1, 2021

Contents

Contents

Introduction:
The Voice of Hope

I am so pleased you have chosen a deeper exploration of my book *Don't Drop the Mic: The Power of Your Words Can Change the World* through your engagement with this study guide. In a world where so many of our institutions are in chaos, the ability to speak with passion and power continues to be among our greatest sources of hope.

The material in this study guide will equip you to grapple with the overarching topic of communication along with my own opinions and experiences. It's up to you to use this guide in the way that best fits your needs, but I certainly hope these pages will complement your understanding and application of the lessons contained in *Don't Drop the Mic*. You may work through the study guide as you read each chapter of the book, use it as a catalyst for fruitful discussion in your small group or book club, or approach it as a devotional companion. The format follows the primary topic from each chapter of the book while adding insight, questions for reflection, and exercises intended to shift the way you think about communicating well.

I've designed this guide to complement the book in addressing several areas and aspects of communication, in addition to many key challenges that often hold communicators back. Knowing this in advance, you may want to read through this guide and the book prior to discussing the material with others so that you have time to process, reflect, and integrate my message. To make sure you get the most out of this experience, I strongly encourage you to address and answer the study questions seriously, and to be as honest and specific as possible in your responses. Remember, effective communication always begins with your own deliberations.

After taking adequate time to absorb and reflect on my particular approaches and opinions regarding the power of words, you will discover that sharing your thoughts and feelings within a group setting can amplify the material's impact. By all means, tell others what activates and inspires you. At the same time, remember that communication is a uniquely individual experience. What excites you may not excite others, but what works for you may also be an anchor for others. So avoid criticism and judgmental comments. Be respectful of your peers and benefit from the blessing of multiple perspectives.

It is my sincere prayer that my words both here and in the book will empower your words to ever-increasing levels of efficacy. As you will see, your voice is needed. So *Don't Drop the Mic!*

CHAPTER I

The Gift of Speech

Having read the Introduction to *Don't Drop the Mic*, you know I was long reluctant to write a book about communication. Speaking and preaching have been foundational components of my life for decades. So has writing. And in recent years I've had the privilege of becoming adept in the world of creating and producing media of many kinds, including movies, music, and more.

In short, I've always been a communicator, and I've always valued the process of effective communication. But *explaining* that process? Teaching it? Making it replicable? Those were areas in which I felt far less confident.

Thankfully, there are people in my life whose character I trust implicitly and whose opinion I value astronomically. Dr. Frank Thomas is such a person. As a seminary professor and a pastor, he shares my love of communication even as he approaches it from a more academic and pedagogical perspective. It was through several encouraging conversations with Dr. Thomas that I began to see a way to share with others how I do what I do as a communicator.

Specifically, I was captivated by the dual meanings behind the phrase *drop the mic*. On the one hand, dropping the mic is a moment of power and triumph—a show of confident knowledge that the words you shared have not been in vain, but have provided intrigue, information, and inspiration for your hearers. On the other hand, to drop the mic can mean literally fumbling an opportunity to step up and share something of value. It's a picture of a wasted opportunity as a communicator.

My goal here, then, is to equip you so that you experience the former—and minimize moments of the latter—as you take advantage of each opportunity to prove the power of words.

1) How would you describe the concept of "communication"? What is it? What is it for?

_____

_____

_____

_____

2) In your own words, what makes communication *effective* rather than *ineffective*?

_____

_____

_____

_____

3) When have you come across an example of effective communication in recent days? How were you affected by that moment?

_____

_____

_____

As I shared in the book, Dr. Martin Luther King Jr. was the first person to awaken my mind about the power of words not just to persuade, not only to influence, but literally to change the world. Watching Dr. King speak so eloquently and so passionately provided me with a living illustration of what I'd been taught in Scripture: "Death and life *are* in the power of the tongue, and those who love it will eat its fruit" (Proverbs 18:21).

That verse was true when it was written, it was true when lived out by Dr. King, and it remains true today. Words carry the power of life and death.

In fact, that verse may be more applicable today than in any prior point in human history. Why? Because communication commands more power and offers more reach today than ever before. It dominates our public attention and saturates our personal interactions. The ability to share of ourselves offers application for career advancement, conflict resolution, establishing relationships, building an audience, delivering a legacy to future generations, and much more.

In short, the sharper our array of communication skills, the more successful we can become in virtually every endeavor.

1) When did you first become aware of the power of words to make a significant impact on the lives of others?

_____

_____

_____

_____

_____

2) Using the scale below, how would you rate your current ability to communicate clearly and effectively?

1	2	3	4	5	6	7	8	9	10

(Terrible communicator)   (Excellent communicator)

3) In which areas of your life does communication play a major role? Check all that apply:

_____ My family

_____ My career

_____ My personal relationships

_____ My hobbies

_____ My relationship with God

_____ Recreation or downtime

_____ Achieving my goals

_____ Finding meaning or purpose

_____ Other:

As we consider the concept of effective communication, we must first think about its ultimate goal. What is the purpose of communicating? Why put in all the effort required to do so—and especially why put in all the effort required to do so effectively?

The answer, in my opinion, is to be understood. The goal of communication is not simply expressing something you believe to be valuable or important. No, the goal of communication is expressing yourself in a way that leads to understanding.

How to achieve that goal is the subject of my book and the remainder of this study guide. However, it is clear right away that our ability to be understood includes a number of important factors. Take language, for example. We are all born into a primary language because of our families, and to a lesser extent because of the communities and broader regions in which we grow up. That primary language becomes our primary tool for communication. Other tools include gestures, emotional expressions, personal gravitas, regional expressions, slang, and more.

Each of these tools are part of our communication repertoire. Each helps us express ourselves in such a way that we can be understood.

Activity: Conduct an experiment regarding your ability to communicate by setting a goal to have an entire conversation with another person without using the word the. Don't allow yourself to use that word—and if you do use it, start the experiment over with your next conversation.

When finished, use the space below to record your thoughts and reactions:

_____

_____

_____

_____

As you grow in your communication skills, you will always be more than the result simply of what you say. You are also influenced incredibly by who you listen to most often, engage with consistently, and spend time around socially. So who are you listening to? And did you ever realize that simply listening to them and dialoguing consistently with them is programming you as a communicator even after you walk away?

Sitting in counsel with those who communicate the way we wish we could can often improve our speaking styles. This sharpening can ultimately improve your economic bottom line, result in invitations to new opportunities, and enhance the number and quality of your relationships. Just as dogs hear high-pitched whistles that fall silent on human ears, our communication style will attract some and be ignored by others. All the more reason to be heard by those whose success you wish to emulate!

1) Who are you listening to? Who are your favorite communicators?

_____

_____

_____

_____

2) Who is listening to *you*?

_____

_____

Another element that's critical in communication is what I think of as *personal style*. No two people on this planet are completely alike, which means no two people will communicate in exactly the same way. We are all individuals—all unique and hand-crafted by our Creator—which means we all express ourselves as individuals.

Looking back at my earliest preaching opportunities, I know my own style was stifled at first because I worked so hard to emulate my favorite communicators. I tried to preach like Dr. King or like the professors I admired most. Quickly, however, I became aware of the simple truth that I could not emulate those giants effectively. I could only succeed as a communicator if I did so as myself.

Therefore, my goal in this material is not to bend you toward a specific style of communication. Rather, I hope to challenge you to consider the forces and factors shaping your own style of communication even as you adapt, adjust, and aspire to new forms of self-expression. In other words, I want to help *you* become the best communicator *you* can be.

1) How would you describe your *style* as a communicator?

_____

_____

_____

_____

2) What goals do you have in mind as you begin this study? What do you want to accomplish through these pages?

_____

_____

_____

_____

CHAPTER 2

Own the Fear Factor

Fear is a universal element in human life. It's something we all experience. What might surprise you is the truth that fear often exerts a positive influence in our lives. Meaning, there is such a thing as "healthy fear"—the feeling that prevents us from jumping off tall buildings, reminds us to run away or take cover when our lives are in danger, or keeps us from taking unnecessary and ultimately destructive risks with our finances.

Yes, fear can be good. At times. Yet in most instances, fear holds us back from that which we would dearly like to achieve or attain. That includes our goals as communicators.

If you want to be a successful communicator, or if you want to move from one degree of success to something greater, you must never allow fear to be the obstacle that hinders your development, experience, and maturity. That includes the fear of failure, the fear of success, the fear of what others might say, the fear of being misunderstood or misaligned, and the fear of criticism.

By this, I don't mean you must never experience fear—that is inevitable. Rather, you must never allow fear to impede or hinder your progress. Owning your fear is the first step in facing it, and facing it is the key to overcoming it.

1) Think back to the last time you stepped out on a limb as a communicator. What emotions did you experience in that moment?

_____

_____

_____

_____

2) What types of communication make you most afraid—oral, written, intimate, public, etc.? Why?

_____

_____

_____

_____

3) When have you successfully faced or overcome a specific fear? How did it happen?

_____

_____

_____

When we look specifically at the fear of communicating, or the fear of expressing ourselves in a public forum, it's critical to remember the stakes. Namely, *someone* will take up the mantle of communication simply because nature abhors a vacuum. If you step back or step away from an opportunity to communicate truth, there will be others more than willing to step forward and offer their own opinions.

Meaning, when we refuse to exercise the power of our words, we allow others to speak for us. We relinquish the power inherent in our own words when we leave them unspoken and unused.

That alone is bad enough, but consider this: Who else is harmed when you allow fear to choke or throttle what you have to say? Remember, you are unique in human history. No other person has the same combination of experience, insight, and wisdom as you. Therefore, no one else can add your voice to the public discourse—only you can do that. And when you refuse, or when you allow fear to keep you silent, you are depriving the world of what only you can contribute.

Activity: Use the space below to record some of the elements that make you unique. These can include specific qualifications, education, transformational life experiences, personal skills or instincts, and so on.

_____

_____

_____

_____

One of the most famous stories in human history began with a man overcoming his fear of communicating—albeit reluctantly. That man's name was

Moses. If you remember the story, you know Moses had a surprising (and potentially inflammatory) encounter with God in which the Almighty commanded him to speak out against Pharaoh of Egypt and demand the release of the Israelites, Moses' own people, who lived as slaves in Egypt.

Moses' first response to that call was soaked in fear: "But Moses said to God, 'Who *am* I that I should go to Pharaoh, and that I should bring the children of Israel out of Egypt?'" (Exodus 3:11). When God promised to be present with Moses and equip him with everything he might need, Moses was still afraid: "Then Moses said to the LORD, "O my Lord, I *am* not eloquent, neither before nor since You have spoken to Your servant; but I *am* slow of speech and slow of tongue" (4:10). Moses was content to allow his physical limitations to silence the power of his words. Even after God offered miraculous displays of power, Moses still resisted: "But he said, "O my Lord, please send by the hand of whom ever *else* You may send" (4:13).

In hindsight, history recognizes Moses as one of the greatest leaders who ever lived. Yet his contribution to the world was almost snuffed out before it got started. Why? Because of fear. May this never be true of us!

1) What are some specific limitations that have restricted or softened your voice?

_____

_____

_____

_____

2) Moses said, "Who am I?" What are the questions that keep you up at night or cause you to feel afraid?

_____

_____

_____

_____

3) Why is communication an essential ingredient for leadership?

_____

_____

_____

_____

When I think about voices being silenced, I can't help my mind being drawn to the terrible and incredible events of 2020. Even now as I write these words, the global COVID-19 pandemic continues to be the dominant story for both local and national news media. And I am reminded once again that, owing to centuries of systemic injustice in my own nation, members of the black community have been silenced by this terrible disease at far greater rates than other groups. We have lost more voices than can be counted, and I am deeply grieved.

In addition, this year has seen an awakening around racial justice the likes of which I have not witnessed since I was a child packed into our living room with the rest of my family, marveling at the words of Dr. King. The spark for that awakening—or perhaps the seed planted in fertile soil—was the murder of George Floyd by police officers in Minneapolis. And not just "Big Floyd," as he was known, but countless other names including Philando Castille, Breonna Taylor, Eric Garner, Michael Brown, Freddie Gray, Tamir Rice, and Atatiana Jefferson, just to name a few.

And as I write these words, I am gratified to see how many are taking advantage of this moment as effective communicators. Millions have risen up to march, to tweet, to text, to e-mail, to cry and shout, and to demand reform, recognition, and restitution. They protested together, wept together, comforted one another, and demanded that others listen to their message—that black lives matter just as much as those of any other human beings. And I must say, it was the diversity of people I saw marching, speaking, and carrying signs that ignited sparks of hope in my soul.

Yet there is more to be done. What I am suggesting could not be simpler, nor could it be more profound: Now is a time to speak. Now is a time for all people of all nations and colors and creeds to rise up and demand that their voices be heard.

Including yours.

1) When have you felt compelled to speak out against a wrong or an injustice? What happened next?

_____

_____

_____

2) What are some different methods of communication employed by those who rose up in protest after the death of George Floyd? Which of those methods did you find most persuasive?

_____

_____

_____

_____

3) Where do you have an opportunity right now to make your voice heard about an issue that matters to you?

_____

_____

_____

_____

CHAPTER 3

Preach but Don't *Preach*

Though I am a preacher by vocation, I am aware that many people have an unfavorable reaction to that word *preach*. Unless they have intentionally sat themselves down for a Sunday sermon, most people don't like being "preached at." Meaning, they don't want to be involuntarily exposed to someone's strong opinions or an unrelenting point of view—which can happen in many settings other than a pulpit. I get that.

Thankfully, the best preachers I know begin with an attitude of humility. They have a genuine desire to teach and bless their hearers, rather than machine-gun their personal preferences and platitudes. More than that, the best preachers are able to match that humble attitude with an effective architecture for communication. That's what we're going to explore together in this session.

When I talk about "architecture" in the realm of communication, I'm talking about the nuts and bolts of assembling an effective message. Just as architects formulate a set of blueprints before they even consider pounding the first nail in a construction project, effective communicators will benefit from thinking through and properly planning their message before they stand up to speak or sit down to write.

This typically involves some form of outline, which usually requires at least a modicum of research. When I begin the initial work of preparing a message—whether that be a sermon, a secular speech, an article, or a book—I start by working to identify the big picture of what I want to say, and then I sift through the relevant information on that topic looking for different points I want to make or details I'd like to share. I refer to this process as "digging up bones" because it's similar to archaeologists uncovering an ankle bone here and a rib there, only eventually combining everything into a more complete skeleton.

1) What's the first thing you typically do to prepare a message you want to communicate with others?

_____

_____

_____

_____

2) What do you like best about researching and doing the prep work for a speech, article, blog post, sermon, and so on?

_____

_____

_____

_____

3) When have you offered up a message without proper preparation? What happened next?

_____

_____

_____

_____

Once you have the "bones" (outline) in place for your message, you should look for what I call "bends." These are the twists and turns inherent in the topic, story, or material you want to share about. You might even think of them as plot twists. They are those areas or moments that carry energy—that pack a punch.

And no, looking for "bends" is not exclusive to sermon preparation. Anything worth talking about will include these pockets of power—these eddies of energy. For example, say you want to deliver a talk about a historical moment. Certainly you will need to do your due diligence in terms of people and places, dates and documents, and facts and figures. Those are the bones. But your message will sharply improve if you can locate some bends within all that data. You might focus on a specific individual or family in order to give a "face" to that period of history. You could read a poignant letter from a soldier to his wife as a supplement to statistics about casualties. That's a bend.

The key is to find the energy. The emotion. The passion. Any presentation— even a quarterly report on your company's top-line budget—can be improved when you find the right bends to bring it to life.

Activity: As you read the following Scripture passage, keep an eye out for the "bones" and the "bends." Record what you find for each category in the spaces below.

⁴⁰So it was, when Jesus returned, that the multitude welcomed Him, for they were all waiting for Him. ⁴¹And behold, there came a man named Jairus, and he was a ruler of the synagogue. And he fell down at Jesus' feet and begged Him to come to his house, ⁴²for he had an only daughter about twelve years of age, and she was dying.

But as He went, the multitudes thronged Him. ⁴³Now a woman, having a flow of blood for twelve years, who had spent all her livelihood on physicians and could not be healed by any, ⁴⁴came from behind and touched the border of His garment. And immediately her flow of blood stopped.

⁴⁵And Jesus said, "Who touched Me?"

When all denied it, Peter and those with him said, "Master, the multitudes throng and press You, and You say, 'Who touched Me?'"

⁴⁶But Jesus said, "Somebody touched Me, for I perceived power going out from Me." ⁴⁷Now when the woman saw that she was not hidden, she came trembling; and falling down before Him, she declared to Him in the presence of all the people the reason she had touched Him and how she was healed immediately.

⁴⁸And He said to her, "Daughter, be of good cheer; your faith has made you well. Go in peace." (Luke 8:40–48)

1) What are the "bones" present in this passage?

_____

_____

_____

_____

2) What are some of the "bends"?

_____

_____

_____

_____

While you are in the preparation stage for your message, it's also critical to spend some time determining the needs of your particular audience. I learned this skill when I began public speaking at venues other than churches. I quickly discovered that what works behind a pulpit on Sunday morning might not work as well—or might not work at all—behind a conference room lectern on a Wednesday afternoon!

First, you'll need to understand who your audience is. Obviously that's more easily accomplished if you are speaking or writing to a specific groups, such as a high school assembly, a company retreat, or an article in an industry-specific publication. Yet even if your audience is more open-ended, you can think through who is most likely to hear your message.

Once you know the *who*, you need to determine the *what*? As in, what is the goal? What does your audience need to hear, or what does your audience expect you to accomplish? The best way to do this is to ask direct questions. Whenever I speak at an event, I spend a significant amount of time on the phone to determine the goals for that event in general, and the goals for my portion specifically. I want to understand the motivations behind my communication, and I especially want to know if any promises have been made or whether any expectations have been set.

And speaking of audiences, it's critical to pay attention to your audience during the actual moment of communication. Of course, this is especially true when you are speaking or presenting in person. This is where you need to be flexible with your outline. If you plan to cover four points, yet you feel a special resonance from your audience during the second point, you may need to scrap your last two ideas and just sit in that powerful moment for as long as possible. Sometimes the most significant and impactful communication occurs when we are willing to be spontaneous and go with the flow.

1) Who are the audiences you communicate to most often?

_____

_____

_____

_____

2) What are the specific needs or motivations of those audiences?

_____

_____

_____

One final note about preparing to communicate your message: Technology can be your best friend or your worst enemy. Yes, the modern bells and whistles of PowerPoint, GIFs, embedded videos, and more can add a satisfying spice to even the most mundane presentations. I recognize the value in technology, and I use it myself in whatever ways are helpful.

But the key word there is *helpful*.

Be careful not to be overly reliant on devices. For one thing, glitches are an ever-present goblin wherever technology can be found. Screens can freeze. Slides can be deleted no matter how assiduously you protect them. Batteries can die. So can microphones. It's also common for speakers and presenters to leave their laptops behind in hotel rooms or in the overhead compartment of their most recent airline flight.

Ask yourself two questions: Can you survive without digital assistance? Can you thrive without it? If you are confident and in charge of your message, then technology will complement your efforts admirably. But if you are relying on the latest and greatest tech as a crutch, chances are good that sooner or later you'll be in for a fall.

1) What are the key elements of technology you rely on as a communicator?

_____

_____

_____

_____

_____

2) Using the scale below, how confident do you feel in your handling of newer tech?

1	2	3	4	5	6	7	8	9	10

(Not confident)   (Very confident)

3) What are practical, actionable ways to master your specific message without relying on technology?

_____

_____

_____

_____

CHAPTER 4

Find the Joint!

One of the truths we need to grapple with when it comes to communication is that words are both mighty and fragile. As I have stated numerous times already, words truly do have the power to change the world. I know that's true because I have experienced it as both a speaker and a hearer. Yet it's also a reality that words can be drowned out. They can be lost. They can be forgotten or ignored.

I fear that today's world is especially hazardous to the impact and impartation of language. Part of that is due to technology. We are constantly crowded by countless screens at every moment of our waking lives. Images are fast becoming our primary mode of expressing meaning, and social media has devolved our speech to the electronic equivalent of monosyllabic grunts and squeals.

Another part of the problem is due to culture. In much of the "developed" world, and especially in my home country of America, politic discourse is a thing of the past. Now we have political shouting. Political accusations. Political grumbling and whining. Perhaps worse, even within the conversations of our closest relationships, communication and conversation are eroding. Most families rarely gather to eat meals or to chat. We text or tweet instead of talk.

For all of these reasons and more, it's critical for us to communicate as efficiently and effectively as possible. We must not let our words go to waste!

1) When was the last time you had a deep and meaningful conversation? How did you feel?

_____

_____

_____

_____

2) What would you identify as specific threats to the medium of communication in today's world?

_____

_____

_____

_____

3) How have you seen changes to that medium from your youth until now?

_____

_____

One of the ways to maximize the efficacy of your communication is to make a direct connection between yourself and your audience. A personal connection. Or to use another term, a relationship.

How does a communicator go about the process of building such a bridge with his or her audience? The first step is to communicate what is important and meaningful to you personally. If you want to connect with your audience, you need to move them. You need to awaken an emotional response or in some other way capture not just their attention, but their appreciation. And I can tell you from experience that it is nearly impossible to move your audience with a theme or subject or idea that you are not moved by yourself.

As I wrote in the book, love is the secret weapon of great speaking. It awakens the speaker and the hearer alike, which opens the door for meaningful connection.

Common ground is another critical element in this idea of connectivity. When you have shared experiences and a shared understanding with your audience, you must use those valuable tools to reinforce the relationship between you. Thus, you must know your audience. You must study and appreciate your audience. And then you will have opportunities—whether writing, speaking, or otherwise—to include illustrations and connection points that establish that intersection between yourself and your audience.

In short, good communication rejects whatever will drive a wedge between us and focuses on what can unite us.

Activity: As you read the passage below from Jesus' Sermon on the Mount, be on the lookout for ways Christ created connectivity between Himself and His audience.

[38]"You have heard that it was said, 'An eye for an eye and a tooth for a tooth.' [39]But I tell you not to resist an evil person. But whoever slaps you on your right cheek, turn the other to him also. [40]If anyone wants to sue you and take away your tunic, let him have *your* cloak also. [41]And whoever compels you to go one mile, go with him two. [42]Give to him who asks you, and from him who wants to borrow from you do not turn away.

[43]"You have heard that it was said, 'You shall love your neighbor and hate your enemy.' [44]But I say to you, love your enemies, bless those who curse you, do good to those who hate you, and pray for those who spitefully use you and persecute you, [45]that you may be sons of your Father in heaven; for He makes His sun rise on the evil and on the good, and sends rain on the just and on the unjust. [46]For if you love those who love you, what reward have you? Do not even the tax collectors do the same? [47]And if you greet your brethren only, what do you do more *than others?* Do not even the tax collectors do so? [48]Therefore you shall be perfect, just as your Father in heaven is perfect." (Matthew 5:43–48)

1) What are some ways Jesus established common ground between himself and his hearers?

_____

_____

_____

_____

2) What are some key areas of common ground between yourself and the audience(s) you are currently serving?

_____

_____

_____

Personal charisma is another element that comes into play with this idea of connectivity. I'm talking about your presence and posture with your audience. I'm talking about the personality you carry and express. In many ways, it's easiest to demonstrate the presence of charisma (or the lack of it!) when you are communicating in person. Yet there are innumerable writers, musicians, YouTube influencers, and other creative types who owe a large part of their success to their ability to display their personality through their chosen medium.

Let me say at this point that it is easy to discount this phenomenon of personal charisma. *It's the information I'm presenting that's important*, you might think, *not the way I present it.* Or, *What I have to say is much more valuable than who I am.* In my experience, these notions are incorrect. If you hire a plumber to fix a leak in your home, there is no need for personal charisma or personal connection within that transaction. There is a problem to be solved, and you simply stand by and allow the professional to solve it.

Communication is different. And it is different precisely because you are attempting to do more as a communicator than solve a problem. You are attempting to understand and be understood. You are attempting to move and be moved. You are attempting to motivate or influence people who are unimaginably complex. Therefore, who you are in that process goes a long way toward whether you will succeed in your goals.

Now, I am not suggesting you attempt to revamp or revitalize your personality in some way. Rather, I am suggesting you be sensitive to what helps create chemistry between yourself and your hearers—and what does not. When you identify something that seems to spark that connection, do more of it. When you identify something that creates a barrier between you and your audience, do less of that. You can work to build chemistry as you develop that connectivity with your hearers.

1) When have you encountered a speaker that made you feel as if he or she were talking directly to you? Why was that?

_____

_____

_____

2) Using the following scale, how confident do you feel in your ability to display charisma or personality in your communication?

1	2	3	4	5	6	7	8	9	10

(No confidence)   (High confidence)

3) When have you connected with an audience in a way that was palpable? How did it happen?

_____

_____

_____

When there is a lack of connectivity between speaker and hearers, I've found one of the more common causes is a lack of awareness on the part of the speaker/communicator in terms of his or her personal brand. Now, I know that word can cause some consternation, but I have found branding to be a critical component in the world of communication.

At the foundation, your brand is the promise you are making to those who hear your words, read your words, or in any way consume "you" through the process of communication. Just as specific plants don't grow well in every climate, your specific brand of communication will not "hit" with every audience. Therefore, it's necessary for you to understand the basic components of that brand, which will allow you to preemptively evaluate a potential audience.

So what is your element? What do you do well? And not just well—what is it you can do better than most? What is it you can share or express better than most? In short, what is it you have to offer to the world, and what are the ways you do best in offering it? Those are core components of your brand.

1) What is your element? What is it you do better than most?

_____

_____

_____

2) If you had to condense your brand into a single sentence, what would you say?

_____

_____

_____

_____

3) Who are some communicators (or even companies) that have been effective in isolating and expressing their core brands?

_____

_____

_____

_____

CHAPTER 5

The Process of Preaching

As a man with a thorough appreciation of food, I've paid special attention over the years to the art and science of cooking. Or more specifically, I've paid special attention to those who excel at the art and science of cooking. I've noticed that some chefs simply have an innate talent that elevates them over their peers—whether those gourmands are serving in five-star restaurants or whipping up family recipes in their household kitchens.

Yet even the most talented chefs have a process they follow as they prepare their culinary creations. No matter your level of natural skill, there will always be vegetables that need chopping, spices that need measuring, and temperatures that need checking. To ignore the scientific process of cooking and rely solely on raw skill is more often than not a recipe for disaster.

The same is true with communication. There are some communicators who simply possess a level of talent unmatched by the vast majority of people, yet that talent will only carry them so far. There is also the process of communicating well—a process that typically includes brainstorming, reflecting, research, outlining, drafting, rehearing, and more.

And so I say this to you: If you desire to be effective in your communication—if your goal is to use your words as tools to change the world—you will ignore the process of communication at your peril.

1) What is your "process" for communicating from beginning to end? How do you typically go about it?

_____

_____

_____

_____

2) What parts of that process are your favorite? Why?

_____

_____

_____

_____

3) What parts of that process do you dislike? Why?

_____

_____

_____

_____

As you consider your own process for communicating, don't overlook the value of experience. There is no quick-fix solution to communicating well, and there is no microwave option for developing the perfect process for communication. Instead, there is the hard work of repetition. Trial and error. Success and evaluation. These are the fertile soil out of which your process will naturally grow.

As I mentioned in the previous chapter, this all starts by identifying what you currently do well. What are your gifts? What opportunities have you been given? What networks or built-in audiences can you access? These are your ingredients for effective communication, and they are the first course when it comes to cooking up a winning process.

Time is another important factor when it comes to the process of communication. Namely, how much do you have? How long can you realistically spend in the different phases of your process before you will need to actually produce a result? Many people have a habit of procrastinating when presented with an opportunity to speak, write, perform, and so on. They wait until the pressure of that last minute pushes them toward productivity. A better approach is to determine how much time you can budget for a specific project, and then hold yourself accountable for spending it wisely.

Conversely, I would never recommend someone reject an opportunity to communicate because of a perceived lack of time. Instead, those moments when you feel rushed are the exact time to trust your process, trust your instincts, trust your natural talent, and go for it!

Activity: Identify a general topic you'd like to share with an audience. This could be a sermon or article you'd like to write, a video you'd like to produce, a speech, etc. Once you know the topic, set a timer for five minutes. After you press "Start," work to develop a basic outline or skeleton for that project. Go as far as you can until the timer beeps.

1) What emotions did you experience while you were "on the clock"?

_____

_____

_____

2) How do you feel about the end result? Why?

_____

_____

_____

To continue on our cooking metaphor for this chapter, transitions are a key ingredient of communication that are often overlooked. What I mean is the specific, intentional methods you use to keep the audience moving with you from point to point, idea to idea, and experience to experience.

Do you remember the last time you flew on an airplane? At some point near the beginning of that flight—often even before takeoff—the captain's voice came over the speakers. She likely introduced herself, then described the elevation at which your flight would take place, and she may even have described different landmarks or cities you would pass along the way to your final destination. In other words, the pilot didn't just tell you where you were going; she explained how you would get there.

As a communicator, you are the one flying the plane. Therefore, you have the responsibility to ensure that your audience follows the course of your flight as smoothly as possible. It's distracting for hearers or readers to be tracking with you on one point, and then all of a sudden hit turbulence as you jump to a completely different idea. And then another. The jolts and jostles will undermine whatever you are trying to say.

In my own experiences as a communicator, I have found it helpful to start out by describing exactly where I intend for the audience to go—what I hope they will learn, experience, and enjoy. I do this by offering a summary or a summation of my primary points. I offer a taste so that they are more prepared to enjoy the full meal at each of its different stages. Such an approach may also be effective for you.

1) How much attention do you pay to transitions and other details in your current communication process?

_____

_____

_____

2) Where can you improve in terms of guiding your audience smoothly through your message or presentation?

_____

_____

_____

Here is the process I use when I prepare a sermon or other speech for public consumption: (1) Study yourself full, (2) Think yourself clear, (3) Pray yourself hot, and (4) Let yourself go. Let me say once again that this should not be *your* process! You are unique, and your preparation for communication should be unique as well. Yet I do want to walk through the four steps outlined above so that you can see a fully formed process in action.

The first step I take in preparing to speak is "studying myself full." Once I've identified a biblical text as the basis of my sermon, I think as broadly as possible about that passage's meaning and application. Part of that study is feeling confident in the original context in which the text was written and the original audience to whom it was given. Another part is studying my audience and understanding the needs and motivations of those who will hear my words. I also spend significant time identifying other Bible passages that connect with that text and color its meaning.

When I say I "think myself clear" as the second step, I mean I think through different ways to communicate the meaning and power of the text with my audience. This is where I put together my outline, including identifying my primary theme, major points, and subpoints. This is also where I identify and explore different metaphors and illustrations that will help illuminate what I am trying to say—or more accurately, what the text is trying to say through me. There is also the matter of arranging the material in a way that makes sense and conveys power.

The third step—"praying myself hot"—is just what it sounds like. With any sermon or speech delivered by me, prayer is present from the very beginning. I saturate each step in prayer. Yet when the time comes to actually deliver the results of that process, I open myself to the work and ministry of the Holy Spirit as an immediate prelude to my presentation.

In the final step, when it's time to speak, I do my best to "let myself go." Meaning, I release any doubts or fears or inhibitions and simply give myself to the moment. I lift my voice to say what needs to be said. I use my body as a tool to complement and characterize my words. Whatever is at my disposal in that moment, I employ it to communicate as clearly and effectively and passionately as possible—because I understand that words can change the world.

1) What adjustments will you make in your process of preparation and presentation as a result of reading this chapter?

_____

_____

_____

_____

2) Which step in the process outlined above seems easiest for you? Which is intimidating? Why?

_____

_____

_____

_____

CHAPTER 6

Where Does It Hurt?

As mentioned earlier, identifying the needs of your audience is a critical component of communication. If you want people to understand you, you must first understand them. And if you want to connect or resonate with your hearers, you must have a firm grasp on their needs and desires.

But how does one actually do that? How can speakers and communicators go about the process of understanding what one person needs, let alone a large and diverse audience? That's what I'll be covering in this chapter. Because regardless of the venue and viewers, knowing how to diagnose your audience's need accurately is vital to your success as a communicator.

Of course, the first—and likely most effective—method of identifying your audience's needs is simply to ask. This can happen during the course of regular conversation with those to whom you are speaking. Feedback is always valuable for communicators, so once you find one or more people willing to share honestly about your performance, be sure to ask what topics, questions, and felt needs are weighing heavily on their hearts. Here's a great question I ask frequently: "What's keeping you up at nights?"

Modern technology also provides many methods for identifying felt needs. If you regularly speak or write to an audience heavy in a specific demographic—black folk, Asian folk, seniors, workers in a specific field or trade, and so on—it's likely you can find surveys and statistics that will help you better understand that group. Or you can set up a poll and get some real, raw data of your own.

The point is this: If you want to identify the needs of your audience, don't be passive. Ask questions and seek answers on your own initiative.

1) How would you answer that question, "What's keeping you up at nights?"

_____

_____

_____

_____

2) What methods have you tried so far to better understand the needs and motivations of your primary audience(s)? What have you learned?

_____

_____

_____

_____

3) What steps can you take in the next few months to begin intentionally and regularly seeking feedback and direct information from your primary audience(s)?

_____

_____

_____

_____

Another great way to identify your audience's felt needs is to watch for results. Meaning, look at the messages or topics or ideas that receive the biggest response from that audience. If people are deeply affected by something you say, and especially if they take the initiative to tell you so, chances are good you've hit a nerve.

Earlier in our ministry, my wife, Serita, and I noticed that many women had questions about healing from the wounds and traumas of their past. Many of these women had experienced abuse of all forms—physical, emotional, sexual—and the scars were still intensely painful. They often asked what resources we could recommend that might lead to a breakthrough.

Well, we couldn't recommend any resources because very few existed at that time. And those that were available were largely of questionable quality. For that reason, I began to speak on that topic from the pulpit. I put together a series I called *Woman, Thou Art Loosed!* It was based on the words of Jesus spoken to a crippled woman on the Sabbath in Luke 13.

The results were tremendous! Each time I preached, the sanctuary was saturated by the healing presence of the Holy Spirit. We saw miracles. We saw freedom. After each message, we received countless requests for audio tapes and sermon transcripts. When we put together a conference specifically on this theme of freedom from bondage, the results were even more incredible. And when I eventually published my own resource for women in need of a spiritual breakthrough, it became a publishing phenomenon that still remains a cornerstone of my ministry to this day.

So we hit a nerve. We identified a powerful need simply by observing the questions and the reactions of our audience. More important, we acted on that need by increasing our communication and offering something of value to meet it.

1) When have you encountered a resource or a message that was exactly what you needed at exactly the right time?

_____

_____

_____

_____

2) In terms of audience response, what are some of your most successful moments as a communicator?

_____

_____

_____

3) What are some of the visible needs or pain points in your community?

_____

_____

As you've seen, some needs are explosive in their obviousness. Yet I've also seen the way many people seek to protect themselves from vulnerability by hiding their needs under a shell of silence. They simply don't talk about it. What then for a communicator seeking to answer the question "Where does it hurt?"

One of the ways to identify these hidden needs is to look for elephants in the room. Look for conflicts or crises that are obviously present yet never addressed. Poverty can be such an elephant, for example. Communities in financial need often deny their own lack out of a desperate desire for dignity. Relational strife is another common elephant in the home—and in the church. When people are not getting along, or when divorce or strife is commonplace, you can be sure there are exposed nerves waiting for the healing salve of truth.

Speaking honestly, the worst thing you can do in the face of such hidden needs is become complicit in the hiding. When people have endured traumas or carried unanswered questions for years, you will only wound them more deeply by pretending "there's nothing to see here."

Activity: As you read the Scripture passage below, be on the lookout for different types of needs present in the story.

> [17]Now it happened on a certain day, as He was teaching, that there were Pharisees and teachers of the law sitting by, who had come out of every town of Galilee, Judea, and Jerusalem. And the power of the Lord was *present* to heal them. [18]Then behold, men brought on a bed a man who was paralyzed, whom they sought to bring in and lay before Him. [19]And when they could not find how they might bring

him in, because of the crowd, they went up on the housetop and let him down with *his* bed through the tiling into the midst before Jesus.

²⁰When He saw their faith, He said to him, "Man, your sins are forgiven you."

²¹And the scribes and the Pharisees began to reason, saying, "Who is this who speaks blasphemies? Who can forgive sins but God alone?"

²²But when Jesus perceived their thoughts, He answered and said to them, "Why are you reasoning in your hearts? ²³Which is easier, to say, 'Your sins are forgiven you,' or to say, 'Rise up and walk'? ²⁴But that you may know that the Son of Man has power on earth to forgive sins"—He said to the man who was paralyzed, "I say to you, arise, take up your bed, and go to your house."

²⁵Immediately he rose up before them, took up what he had been lying on, and departed to his own house, glorifying God. ²⁶And they were all amazed, and they glorified God and were filled with fear, saying, "We have seen strange things today!" (Luke 5:17–26)

1) What are the obvious, external needs present in this passage?

_____

_____

_____

_____

_____

2) What are the hidden, internal needs evident among the different characters of this story?

_____

_____

_____

_____

I would be remiss if I did not take this opportunity to address the extreme explosion of need that has taken place not only in America throughout 2020, but also across the world. I am speaking again of the protests and elevated awareness of racial justice issues that have arisen after so many documented cases of police abusing their power against black people in particular.

When you think about it, protests are a powerful medium of communication. When tens of thousands—and even hundreds of thousands—of men and women of all ages and colors join together to raise their voices and their banners high, people must take notice. The message cannot be ignored. Even the violence and looting that have accompanied these times is a form of communication, although in my opinion one that is less effective and more destructive.

Any communicator worth their salt must take notice of such a moment. Why? Because people are literally taking to the streets to declare their needs to the world. The need to be valued. The need to be respected. The need to be protected. And perhaps most encouraging of all, people have taken to the streets to express their desire for *others* to be valued, respected, and protected.

These are universal longings, and I can say without doubt they apply directly to your audience. So the question becomes: What will you do about it?

1) How have you been personally affected by the recent uprisings and marches in opposition to racial injustice?

_____

_____

_____

_____

2) Where do you have opportunities to meet the expressed needs of those seeking justice and freedom from oppression?

_____

_____

_____

_____

CHAPTER 7

Every Shot Is the Only One You Have

I have been making the case throughout this study (and the corresponding book) that words carry incredible power. Language carries incredible power. That's why the act of communication is so important, because your speech can change the world.

During my discussions with communicators of different levels over the years, I've found that most really do believe in the power of words and the potential for speech to instigate lasting change. However, I've also discovered a pervasive feeling among communicators that such moments are rare. In fact, there are many who speak and write under the impression that they will have only a few opportunities over the course of their life to really communicate in a way that makes a difference.

Communicators often struggle with the idea that much of what they say, write, or present will have little or no impact. Perhaps they see a small number of people in their field with large and influential platforms, and they carry the impression that only such people can wield real influence. Or perhaps they feel the "stars must align" at some perfect moment for their message to truly get across and gain some traction.

Based on my own experiences, I advise any person with a message to treat any and every opportunity to share that message as a sacred calling. A once-in-a-lifetime opportunity. Because as I've witnessed personally, even the most seemingly mundane and routine moment can create history.

1) What are some assignments or projects you've participated in recently that just felt like you were going through the motions?

_____

_____

_____

_____

2) How would you describe the impact you've made so far as a communicator? Where do you see fruit?

_____

_____

_____

_____

3) Using the scale below, how convinced are you that your words—your opportunities to share and understand and be understood—can create real change?

1	2	3	4	5	6	7	8	9	10

(Unconvinced)   (Convinced)

For communicators seeking a breakthrough, the best advice I can offer is to treat every opportunity as the cusp of your break-out moment. By that, I mean you should view even the most mundane moment—whether it be an article or an event or a substitute sermon or a Zoom presentation or even taking the mic at your local community association—as your chance to shine.

First and foremost, you should prepare for every opportunity as if it were your best opportunity. Put in the work. Put in the research. Put in the time to practice and rehearse and seek feedback so that when the moment comes, you can nail it to the wall. Or put another way, so you can drop the mic.

The reality is that opportunity begets opportunity. One door opening often leads to another. And another. And another. That's the nature of networking and word of mouth. That's the nature of communication! How unfortunate, then, if you skip that first door because it does not seem worth your while.

In addition to preparation, never let any obstacle drag you down in the actual moment of delivery. Don't let fear keep you from delivering your best. Don't let boredom or bitterness color your presentation. Certainly never allow arrogance or pride to communicate through your face or your words that you believe yourself above this moment and this audience.

Instead, treat every shot as if it were your best shot at success. Because it may be!

1) Do you categorize some opportunities as bigger or more important than others? Why or why not?

_____

_____

_____

_____

2) What are some ways to build accountability into your preparation process so that you can avoid a lackluster performance?

_____

_____

_____

_____

Another key to making the most of every speaking opportunity is to put some extra focus, preparation, and performance into your first sixty to ninety seconds. They say you never get a second chance to make a first impression, and they are right. So spend some extra time preparing to make that impression a good one.

Every time you speak or present yourself in front of others, you are beginning that moment with a degree of distance between yourself and the audience. There is a barrier of sorts in place—you are onstage or behind the podium, and they are in the chairs. You are an individual and they are a crowd. You are offering something and they are expected to receive it.

What's critical to understand is that the first moments of your presentation will have an effect on that distance—on that barrier. Either you will lessen the space between yourself and your audience, or you will increase it. You'll either break down the barrier between you or add a few more layers.

Similarly, most of the people in your audience will be ready to engage with you at least at some level. They will participate in the act of communication—at least at first. It's within those first few moments that they will decide whether to broaden or narrow that engagement. If you draw them in and give them a reason to connect, they will step toward you. If you keep them at a distance or if you straight up underperform, they will resign themselves to spending the next thirty or sixty or ninety minutes in a state of polite endurance.

Always remember, it's up to you to convince the audience that what you have to say is worth their time, not the other way around.

1) How do you typically approach the first moments of a speaking engagement or presentation?

_____

_____

_____

_____

2) What are some physical signs or cues that audience members are connecting with what you are sharing?

_____

_____

_____

_____

3) What are some signs or cues that show audience members have disconnected?

_____

_____

_____

_____

_____

One word we haven't focused on extensively yet in this study guide is *authenticity*. In my opinion, authenticity is critical to effective communication. That's because authenticity plays a huge role in many of the concepts we've already explored—the idea of being understood, of connecting and intersecting with your audience, of establishing an effective brand, and more.

The first step in authenticity as a communicator is to genuinely believe what you are saying—and to *believe in* what you are sharing. People generally don't like being sold something, and people can generally tell when a communicator is more interested in "results" than in actually making a personal connection. Yes, there are a lot of speakers out there who can rightly be accused of "selling" their message, but I've observed that most of them get called out in the end. The crowd will eventually smell a fraud.

If it's bad news that your audience will pick up on a poorly prepared or inauthentic presentation, the good news is that the opposite is also true. When you genuinely put in the work to offer something valuable to your listeners— which, after all, is a matter of showing respect for their time—they will see it. When you have a real and deep-seated passion for the material you are presenting, they will know it.

So if you take advantage of every opportunity in that way, you will reap the dividends of your hard work and belief. Count on it!

Activity: If you are able to turn on the television for a few minutes, find some commercials to watch. What are some common elements present when someone is trying to "sell" you on a product or an idea?

CHAPTER 8

Learn the Grammar of Body Language

Take a moment to imagine the following scenario: You're bored out of your mind in the middle of a presentation. This could be anything from a quarterly revenue projection delivered by your company's CFO to a late-night church service. But wherever you are and whoever is up there onstage, it's not working. You're not tracking. You're not even sitting in a comfortable chair. And you are well aware of the fact that there are still at least another thirty minutes to go.

Try to put yourself in that room. What would be going through your mind? How would you be attempting to occupy yourself. Or perhaps more likely, how would you attempt to demonstrate that you were paying close attention?

I want you to pay special attention to your body language in such a moment. What would your feet be doing? Your legs? How would you try to sit? Could you stay in the same position for a long time, or would you have to shift around? What about your hands? What would they be doing? And if you began to have a difficult time staying awake, how you would solve that problem?

I hope I haven't scared you (or scarred you!) with this little exercise. But I think it's necessary to illustrate that one of the most important aspects of communication is body language. That includes both voluntary and involuntary gestures, postures, facial expressions, and more.

1) Use the space below to record your answers to the questions above. How would your body respond in a situation where you were bored out of your mind?

_____

_____

_____

_____

2) In general, do you do a good job of reading other people's body language? Explain.

_____

_____

_____

3) What are some ways you currently incorporate or plan for body language in your presentations or performances?

_____

_____

I'm sure you've heard the expression *Dress for success*. What about *What you see is what you get*? There are countless other colloquialisms for the way our outward appearance influences the way others perceive us, but they pretty much all point in the same direction: Whether we admit it or not, we often *do* judge a book by its cover.

The first step in using body language to enhance (rather than detract from) your communication is to manage the way you look. Specifically, the way you dress and present yourself. Now, I am not necessarily suggesting you dress up in a suit and tie for every occasion. It is possible to be overdressed, not to mention undercomfortable.

What I do suggest is that you take some time to consider how you want to portray yourself to your audience. What is the message you want to communicate with your "look"? Next, it's important to look comfortable and confident whenever you speak or present in front of others. For that to happen, you need to actually *feel* comfortable, which means don't wear too tight collars or too skinny jeans. You also need to *feel* confident, which means you should select an outfit that both flatters your physicality and accentuates your attitude.

Another item to consider when selecting your wardrobe is what the members of the audience are likely to be wearing. Don't be informal in a formal setting, or vice versa. Don't go for laughs when the mood will be somber. Take into account the level of professionalism that will be demonstrated by your peers and expected by your hearers—and when in doubt, it's better to be overdressed than underdressed.

Finally, I do recommend you take some time to try on your outfit or ensemble before the actual day of your event. That may seem like an annoyance, but you don't have to be Janet Jackson to experience a wardrobe malfunction. Better safe than sorry.

Activity: Take a few moments to go through several photos of yourself. Identify images where you look comfortable, and where you remember feeling comfortable and confident. Then identify images where you look uncomfortable or out of place. Use the space below to reflect on these observations.

1) What were some of the outfits in which you looked and felt the best? What do those outfits have in common?

_____

_____

_____

_____

2) What were you wearing in pictures that did not come across as well? What would you identify as the problem in those photos?

_____

_____

_____

_____

3) Who can you rely on for honest counsel when it comes to looking your best and dressing for success?

_____

_____

_____

_____

It's easy to forget that your voice—the auditory aspect of your speech—is included in this idea of body language. Not the words you say, of course; that is just regular "language." Rather, I'm talking about the *way* you say what you say. The pitch of your voice. Your overall volume and the way you fluctuate from quiet to loud to quiet again. The passion and power present in your voice, and the way you use periods of silence. All of these are critical components of communication.

In fact, you might be surprised to learn that oral communication has many advantages over the written word when it comes to precision and control. It's difficult to type sarcastically, for example, but you can convey a whole new depth of meaning to your words by allowing them to drip and drawl with derision or disdain. An exclamation point is just a line on top of a dot, but a passionate SHOUT! at just the right moment can grab your hearers' attention and never let it go.

For these reasons, be aware of the ways your voice can serve as a valuable tool for effective communication. Actually, strike that. Don't just be aware of your voice—*relish* your voice. Luxuriate in the ups and downs, the presses and pauses, the depth and richness of your vocal range. Practice using the instrument of your voice to its fullest and most impactful effect.

1) Use the scale below to show how often you rely on your voice as a vocal instrument during speeches or presentations.

1	2	3	4	5	6	7	8	9	10

  (Never)   (Always)

2) Among the speakers you admire, who does a great job of modulating and managing their voice to capture and keep attention?

_____

_____

_____

_____

Now let us turn our attention to what people typically think of when they use the term *body language*. That would include physical posture, gestures, facial expressions, the use of hands, and so on. Each of those items are key elements in your communication. Yet each of those items can also be overdone.

I like to think of body language as the herbs and spices of communication. When used correctly, they can season your speech in a way that makes everything better, more memorable, and much more effective. When used incorrectly, however—whether by being ignored or overindulged—body language can overpower your presentation and leave you looking like a third-rate clown at your child's birthday party.

What does it look like for you to use body language effectively? I cannot say. Remember, communication is unique to the communicator. I like to be active with my body whenever I speak. I march around our stage at the Potter's

House during services there. I clap my hands to emphasize key points. I lean my head back and look at the rafters when I need to raise my voice. All of that has worked for me, but what works for me may not work for you.

One way to identify what works for you is to record your speeches and presentations, then watch the replay with a critical eye. What looks forced? What looks natural? Are there moments during your speech that feel dull or dragging? Maybe it's time to insert some hand gestures or other body language to give the audience a focal point. Are there times when you get a little bit out of control with your hands? Maybe that's a signal to grab the lectern and lean toward your hearers.

The key is to identify the methods that work for you and keep you comfortable. Remember, you ignore body language at your peril as a communicator. It's critical to use every tool in your communication toolbox!

1) How can you tell when you are relying too much on body language?

_____

_____

_____

2) What are some of your favorite ways to employ your body as a speaker? What do you communicate with those gestures or methods?

_____

_____

_____

CHAPTER 9

The Pregnant Pause

As I noted in my book, negative space is a requisite aspect of any artistic expression. It's the "white space" in a picture or photo or work of art—the empty area or margin not dedicated to the focal point of that picture or photo or work of art. Visual artists use negative space as a way to highlight and emphasize the core of their work. It adds depth and dimension to what they are trying to show.

In a similar way, silence acts as the negative space for oral speeches or presentations. Silence both bookends and emphasizes our words. It adds depth and emotion to what we say and how we say it. Therefore, though such a statement may sound oxymoronic, silence is an essential element of communication.

In fact, what I hope to show you in this chapter is that silence is a language unto itself. Silence lubricates the ideas, examples, and anecdotes shared in communication. It can create tension and suspense, provide emphasis and direction, open space for reflection and application, and add value, honor, and respect. Knowing how to maximize silence also enhances your ability to communicate with language as well as without.

Silence is a gift, a tool, a frame, a relationship, and an invitation. So let's take a closer look together at how it works and how to maximize it through your speech.

Activity: Grab a timer and set it for two minutes. Once you press "Start," spend those two minutes in as complete a silence as you are able. Then record your thoughts through the questions below.

1) How did you feel during this period of intentional silence? What emotions did you experience?

_____

_____

_____

2) Where did your mind go during that period of silence? What did you think about?

_____

_____

_____

3) How did you respond when the silent period was over? Were you more relieved or disappointed? Why?

_____

_____

_____

_____

_____

Whenever I speak in front of an audience, I consider that moment to be a conversation between myself and my hearers. Of course, I do most of the talking, but that doesn't mean it's a monologue. Rather, every time I open my mouth, I do so in the fervent hope and expectation that my words will cause a response within the minds and the hearts of those who hear what I came to say.

That's why silence is critical to the act of communication—because our hearers need time and space in order to meditate on what we say and formulate their own responses.

Think of it like an actual conversation. If you and I were engaged in a dialogue, but I just kept talking and talking without every pausing for you to reply—that would be very unsatisfying for at least one of us. It's the pauses and quiet moments that allow two or more voices to share the same conversation.

Well, the same idea comes into play when we speak. If we motor-mouth our way through a presentation without ever stopping, without pausing and allowing a little silence in the room, the audience will have no time to give any consideration to what we've said. Their ears will be functioning but their minds will be on autopilot.

Of course, the amount of silence you allow may depend on your total amount of available time. That's why pace is another critical component of communication. If you've got a long message and a long time to share it, you can be more liberal in your use of pauses and silence. If your time is short, however, you may need to employ shorter and fewer moments for reflection.

1) Do you agree or disagree that speeches and presentations should be viewed in terms of a conversation? Explain.

_____

_____

_____

_____

2) When you speak, how often do you typically allow pauses or moments of silence? Is it intentional?

_____

_____

_____

_____

3) How do you incorporate pacing into your planning and preparation process?

_____

_____

_____

Silence is also useful as a way of adding emphasis to your message. If you've done the work of researching not only your presentation but also your audience, you'll go into a speech with a good idea of which moments or points or ideas will resonate well with your hearers. So when you stop for a few seconds before delivering that moment or point or idea, you'll give a cue to the audience that something good is coming their way.

This is important because any good speech or vocal performance will rise and fall in intensity.

As you share your message, you're building a series of points and counterpoints, ideas and illustrations, lessons and applications. You are leading your audience upward toward the peak of the mountain, which is the crux of your message.

Well, anyone who has ever hiked a real mountain knows you can't take it all in one go! There need to be periods of rest. Moments where you stop and enjoy the view. Moments where you catch your break and grab some water. Then, refreshed, you continue on the journey.

Silence is your way of showing the audience that you've reached one of those stopping places. This will usually coincide with the main points or key illustrations of your outline. You want to give everyone a chance to consider the ground they've covered before they begin marching once again toward the peak.

1) Which speakers have you heard who were masters in using silence?

_____

_____

_____

_____

2) How much should speakers plan these "stopping points," and how much should they be natural?

_____

_____

_____

_____

Some of my favorite action movies feature many cliffhanger moments. You know what I'm talking about, right? The hero bursts into a room bristling with bad guys, only to take a bullet and go down. Or the hero is literally hanging from the edge of a building or a sheer rock face. And then, just when things look bleakest, the film cuts away to another scene focusing on other actors—leaving you to wonder, *What happened? Is she hurt badly? Will he fall?*

For all kinds of storytelling, cliffhanging moments are designed to create suspense and engagement on the part of the audience. We can accomplish the same effect during an oral presentation by using silence. As you build toward a key moment or a poignant point in your speech, the audience will feel the intensity building. They will know the truth is coming. Therefore, if you use a pregnant pause before delivering that key moment or poignant point, you will draw them in and build anticipation for what's next.

Now the length of your pregnant pause is important. Too short and you won't actually accomplishing anything because the audience won't notice. Too long and you'll drift into an awkward moment. The right length for a pregnant pause is typically one or two seconds. If the audience is really hanging on your every word, you can build a great amount of anticipation by extending a silent moment as you walk across the stage, grab a drink of water, or—if you're anything like me—use a towel to wipe away the sweat on the back of your neck.

1) In addition to silence, what are some other ways of adding moments of suspense to your speech or presentation?

_____

_____

_____

2) In your experience, how can you tell when a moment of silence is stretching out too far?

_____

_____

_____

3) What are some other ways to build in "practical" moments of silence (such as drinking some water)?

_____

_____

Finally, I would be doing a disservice to this topic if I did not address one of the biggest and baddest banes of a speaker's journey: awkward silence. Most of the time, this is unintentional silence. When you forget your place, for example, or when your PowerPoint isn't working the way you planned and you need to make some tweaks or changes to the presentation.

Awkward silence is a killer for quality communication. Whatever groove you were operating in is all of a sudden a minefield. Whatever goodwill or appreciation you had built up with your audience goes out the window like a breeze. And the terrifying moments you spend trying to regain your composure or get back in the game will likely make the remainder of your speech all the more difficult to land well.

That's why I cannot emphasize enough the need to perfect your process for preparation. Do everything you can on the front end to make sure there will be no glitches or gaffes in the moment of your speech. That means checking and double-checking any technology, rehearsing your delivery until you are bursting with confidence, and perhaps even preparing an emergency joke or conversation starter as a "break glass in case of emergency" tool.

One final note on awkward silence: It can also rear its ugly head when your material is not where it needs to be. For example, if you build up momentum for a specific point—perhaps even using silence to increase the tension—but then that point is obvious or overly complicated, you will feel the awkward moment of a stillborn delivery. The same can be true of a joke that falls flat. When you experience those moments during a speech or presentation, be sure to perform an autopsy afterward. Don't assume everything will be better next time with a different audience. Rather, do the work of fixing what is broken.

1) When have you endured a moment of awkward silence during a speech or presentation? What emotions did you experience during and after?

_____

_____

_____

_____

2) Using the scale below, how confident do you feel when it comes to repairing a "broken" moment during a presentation?

1	2	3	4	5	6	7	8	9	10

(No confidence)   (Fully confident)

3) Who can help you get better at performing surgery on your presentations?

_____

_____

_____

_____

CHAPTER 10

Tour Guides and Trailblazers

As I mentioned earlier in this study guide, the best moments of communication are those that create an intersection between you and your audience, whichever form that audience may take. There needs to be a connection. Even a relationship. In order to make that happen, you must understand your audience—who they are, what motivates them, what felt needs they have brought with them to this moment of intersection, and so on.

But you must also understand yourself! If there is to be any connectivity between yourself and your audience, you need to have a firm grasp of who you are as a communicator and what you can offer to those who will take the time to listen, read, or otherwise engage with anything you have to say.

Part of that understanding should include those who have gone before you in your preferred medium of communication. Sir Isaac Newton spoke of his greatest accomplishments as "standing on the shoulders of giants." The same is true for you. Whether consciously or unconsciously, you have been influenced by great communicators of the past and present. Therefore, your style, delivery, and overall performance will bear some resemblance to those giants.

In my experience, it's better to have a conscious understanding of these influences; that way you can maximize the positive without unintentionally becoming rote or unoriginal.

1) Who are some great communicators from the past that you admire? How have they influenced you?

_____

_____

_____

_____

2) Who are some great communicators from the present that you have followed in your preferred medium? What makes them great?

_____

_____

_____

_____

3) Where would you like to draw the line between being inspired by those giants and actively imitating them?

_____

_____

_____

In the book, I described how a trip to London actively revealed to me the difference between a *dilettante* and a *docent*. I met the dilettante during a bus tour of the city. I was expecting an intellectually invigorating exploration of the metropolis, but what I received instead was a bored and uninspired gent simply reading from a script of predictable provender.

Thankfully, I had a much better experience the next day with a docent. As explained to me, a docent is someone with an active and deep expertise of a specific subject. In many colleges and universities around the world, a docent falls just below the rank of professor in terms of intellectual rigor and understanding. I was energized by the way my docent offered me a personal and personalized tour of the city, even taking delight when I asked questions and wanted to dive deeper into different rabbit holes.

As a communicator, you face a similar choice: Will you be a dilettante or a docent? Meaning, will you play it safe with your audiences and be content to simply repeat and rehash the same old material? Or will you go deeper? Will you cultivate an expertise not only in the subject matter you explore, but also in the lives, dreams, and motivations of those who choose to explore it with you?

Here's another way of approaching this question: Do you delight your audiences, or do you merely inform them? That's the key difference between a docent and a dilettante, and that's something only you can choose to pursue.

1) How would you answer that question: Do you delight your audiences or merely inform them? Explain.

_____

_____

_____

2) What causes speakers or other communicators to "play it safe"?

_____

_____

_____

_____

3) What are some practical steps you can take to avoid that temptation and instead determine to delight your hearers?

_____

_____

_____

_____

I also described in the book how a visit to a dude ranch out West showed me the difference between tour guides and trailblazers. Both of those titles have obvious meanings. Tour guides stick to predetermined paths; they look at the same landmarks and spout out the same material day in and day out. Trailblazers, on the other hand, specialize in the new. They intentionally work off the beaten path and create new trails that others can follow.

Let me ask you, then, are you a tour guide or a trailblazer as a communicator? Do you stick to what's safe and travel the same ground as those who came before you? (This is an especially common temptation for pastors, since there is no avenue of the biblical text or the ins and outs of the Christian life that has not already been explored.) Or do you break open new vistas and new opportunities for discovery?

In my opinion, the best communicators are trailblazers. That means being willing to tackle topics that have previously been taboo. It means taking old ideas and reimagining them in a new way. It means not being content with the established methods of delivery, but instead finding your own way and your own voice that is distinct and definitive. And that means being willing to take risks and even cause offense.

1) As a communicator, are you more of a tour guide or a trailblazer? Explain.

_____

_____

_____

_____

2) Look again at what it means to be a trailblazer above. Which of those descriptions excites you most? Why?

_____

_____

_____

_____

3) Which of those descriptions makes you nervous? Why?

_____

_____

_____

_____

Let me offer a fair warning before we close out this chapter: Choosing to be a trailblazer in your communication may cause you some grief. Or more realistically, it will *likely* cause you some grief. That's because you can't break open new ideas and new methods without offending somebody. It is simply inevitable. As Taylor Swift so rightly declared, "Haters gonna hate."

This is an especially grievous fear for pastors. Those of us who stand behind the pulpit each week have a responsibility to serve as shepherds to our people. We care for them. Tend them. Defend them. And when necessary, try to move them away from a destructive path. It can be difficult, therefore, for pastors to knowingly and willingly share a topic or a truth that will likely cause pain. Or rejection.

Yet even beyond pastors, any person who endeavors to understand and to be understood—meaning, any person who chooses to communicate—is putting themselves at risk. Any audience can contain those dour individuals who like to find fault. Anytime you share the truth, and especially anytime you attempt to lead others toward something new, there will be those who prefer to remain in the mud of their own ignorance.

To communicate effectively, then, you must be willing to take those risks. Because the reward is worth it.

Activity: The prophets of the Old Testament were powerful trailblazers, and they often paid for it with their lives. Read the following passage from Ezekiel and then answer the questions below.

¹"You also, son of man, take a clay tablet and lay it before you, and portray on it a city, Jerusalem. ²Lay siege against it, build a siege wall against it, and heap up a mound against it; set camps against it also, and place battering rams against it all around. ³Moreover take for yourself an iron plate, and set it *as* an iron wall between you and the city. Set your face against it, and it shall be besieged, and you shall lay siege against it. This *will be* a sign to the house of Israel.

⁴"Lie also on your left side, and lay the iniquity of the house of Israel upon it. *According* to the number of the days that you lie on it, you shall bear their iniquity. ⁵For I have laid on you the years of their iniquity, according to the number of the days, three hundred and ninety days; so you shall bear the iniquity of the house of Israel. ⁶And when you have completed them, lie again on your right side; then you shall bear the iniquity of the house of Judah forty days. I have laid on you a day for each year.

⁷"Therefore you shall set your face toward the siege of Jerusalem; your arm *shall be* uncovered, and you shall prophesy against it. ⁸And surely I will restrain you so that you cannot turn from one side to another till you have ended the days of your siege.

⁹"Also take for yourself wheat, barley, beans, lentils, millet, and spelt; put them into one vessel, and make bread of them for yourself. *During* the number of days that you lie on your side, three hundred and ninety days, you shall eat it. ¹⁰And your food which you eat *shall be* by weight, twenty shekels a day; from time to time you shall eat it. ¹¹You shall also drink water by measure, one-sixth of a hin; from

time to time you shall drink. ¹²And you shall eat it *as* barley cakes; and bake it using fuel of human waste in their sight."

¹³Then the LORD said, "So shall the children of Israel eat their defiled bread among the Gentiles, where I will drive them." (4:1–13)

1) What risks was Ezekiel taking by delivering this message?

_____

_____

_____

_____

2) How did Ezekiel function as a trailblazer in terms of his delivery of that message?

_____

_____

_____

_____

CHAPTER 11

Sound Check

The act of communication typically involves motion. If that sounds strange, what I mean is that communicators are typically going somewhere. We don't speak or write or perform simply to be onstage for a few moments or to get some clicks on our most recent posts. Instead, we have a goal in mind—a destination. And the best communicators understand they need to take their audiences with them on that journey.

How do you accomplish that? One necessary step is maintaining the attention of your audience. Of course, part of this has to do with the material in your message. You'll have difficulty maintaining your audience's attention if you don't have anything worthwhile to say. But another part is connected to your delivery—to the medium through which you transmit your message.

As a preacher, I've learned to have a gentle touch with my audience. I want to guide them on a journey with me, but I don't want to force them anywhere. So I typically resist any large shows of force while I'm speaking or writing. I make a point not to bully, berate, or browbeat my hearers.

I have also found that allowing my personality to shine through the message is a great way to keep my audience's attention. I am a gregarious person. I enjoy fun and laughter and joy. Therefore, I allow those elements to become part of my communication. Often speakers and writers allow themselves to be dragged down by the misapprehension that communication is supposed to be serious and stolid, like an academic lecture. On the contrary, I have found the most success as a communicator when I have a good time, which means it's likely my audience will have a good time as well.

1) What are some keys you've discovered to keeping an audience's attention?

_____

_____

_____

2) What are some particular challenges to engaging your audience in the communication medium you prefer?

_____

_____

_____

3) Using the scale below, how well do you allow your personality to infuse your communication?

1	2	3	4	5	6	7	8	9	10
(Not well)								(Very well)	

Another key to maintaining your audience's attention is to communicate in a way that is timeless. And by "timeless," I mean finding a balance between hip and hopeless.

Audiences will have a difficult time staying engaged with a communicator who is out of touch. Meaning, one who is stuck in the past. For that reason, it's important to keep yourself up to date with all manner of topics, including technology, the latest news, popular culture, and general current and global events. You will have a better chance of keeping your audience's attention if they see you as relevant and informed.

However, it's also possible to tip the scales too far in the direction of relevance. This happens when a communicator "tries too hard." They use slang that is obviously uncomfortable or unnatural for them. They try to be on the razor's edge of technology without actually understanding the best way to use their various gadgets and gizmos. They name-drop young celebrities and try to incorporate fresh music or videos.

All these efforts are likely to cause younger generations to respond with, "Okay Boomer."

Once again, the right goal is to find the proper balance between ancient and trendy. That usually starts with being yourself, and then doing the appropriate research and preparation. But it also includes focusing on topics and methods that rise above the typical trends of culture.

Activity: Take five or ten minutes to watch a few YouTube videos that are popular or trending. Answer the follow questions to unpack that experience.

1) How did the content originators of those videos do in finding a balance between trendy and out of touch?

_____

_____

_____

2) What did you like most about the videos? What did you dislike?

_____

_____

_____

3) How would you describe a good balance for you when it comes to being "timeless" for your methods of communication and your audience?

_____

_____

_____

There are a great many communicators I both know and admire who struggle with perfectionism. I find that more than understandable! After all, the act of communication is nothing without an audience, and any audience of any size will give feedback to the communicator. It's easy to become paralyzed by perfectionism when that feedback is less than ideal.

Unfortunately, a drift toward perfectionism is another barrier that can prevent you from meaningful engagement with your audience.

Depending on the circumstances of your communication, it's usually easy to determine whether you have succeeded overall. People were hanging on your every word, the article generated more page views than any of your other writing, you received a standing ovation, and so on. What's more difficult, however, is determining *why* things don't work the way you intended them to work. *Why did that joke fall flat? Why did I lose the jury? Why were the students so uninterested today?*

As I mentioned before, performing an autopsy on an unsuccessful attempt at communication can lead to valuable results. There will come a time, however, when you will need to simply let things go. Not every communicative journey will lead to connection. There will be mishaps and mess-ups. Sometimes the best way to respond in those moments is to refuse to allow your internal critic to paralyze you with hopelessness or despair.

1) Use the scale below to identify how much you struggle with perfectionism.

1	2	3	4	5	6	7	8	9	10
(Deep struggle)							(No struggle)		

2) Who can you depend on to give you honest and accurate feedback?

_____

_____

_____

_____

One final methodology I want to explore on this topic of keeping an audience engaged is focusing on your feelings as a communicator. In fact, that may be the most important factor! That's because feelings and emotions are at the heart of communication. People are listening to more than your words when you open yourself to share something important—they are also listening to your heart.

In my opinion, there are far too many people in today's world who approach the act of communication as an academic exercise. They focus on facts and figures. Or they hit the right notes or strike the right poses without any emotion behind the experience. Such performances typically leave me unsatisfied.

On the other hand, it's also possible for communicators to go all in on the emotion without actually having anything worthwhile to say or display. They pour out feelings all over the stage or the page, yet there's no substance with it. No opportunity for learning or growth or genuine change. Effective communicators avoid both of these extremes.

So another line you must tiptoe along as a communicator is allowing your feelings to shine through without drowning the audience. How this actually works is different for each person. The key is to learn control, which comes through practice and experience.

1) Do you lean more toward overexpression or underexpression when it comes to your emotions?

_____

_____

_____

_____

2) Why are feelings and emotions an important element in communication?

_____

_____

_____

_____

3) When have you allowed your feelings to show through in a way that demonstrated balance and control? How did the audience respond?

_____

_____

_____

_____

CHAPTER 12

Keep Your Cool When the Mic Is Hot

In the world of media production, a "hot mic" is simply a microphone that is turned on and recording. Because interviewees and other performers often require multiple takes to get a segment perfect, the audiovisual team will often leave the mic running between those attempts. That has led to many embarrassing moments when celebrities, news anchors, or even presidential candidates let something slip when they didn't know they were being recorded.

I also think of the microphone as "hot" because of the pressure it brings. Whenever you step up to a microphone or stand up before an audience—or whenever you get ready to hit "Publish" on an article or other element of content creation—you are making yourself more vulnerable than many can tolerate. There is no hiding from the mic. The heat is on.

For these reasons, I counsel communicators to be as authentic as possible during any and all hot-mic moments. The more you try to create a persona or "manage" yourself during public moments, the more shock and confusion your audience will feel when one of your private moments gets blown up for all to see. The more authenticity you bring to your role as a communicator, the more comfortable you will feel in your own skin, even when the mic is on and everyone is listening.

Over the years, I've learned there's no substitute for the connection that comes from sharing your authentic self with others. Most people can tell if you're faking authenticity. They not only wonder what your motive is for such deception but also doubt your credibility. And when your credibility is in question, then you've compromised your authority and given your audience reason to distrust you and your message. So why bother? Authenticity is ultimately worth the risk.

1) What are some memorable hot-mic moments that caught your attention in the past?

_____

_____

_____

_____

2) How do you typically handle the pressure of offering yourself to public exposure?

_____

_____

_____

_____

3) What does the idea of "authenticity" mean to you? How do people display it?

_____

_____

_____

_____

Many times throughout this study guide, I have mentioned the importance of preparation and maintaining your process as the starting point of communication. It is critical to your success! However, when it comes to maintaining authenticity and being real in front of an audience, spontaneity is another useful tool in your toolbox.

Now, I need to mention that there are speech experts out there who severely frown on spontaneity during the communication process. Why? Because it takes things out of your control. Nevertheless, I have found that the benefits of spontaneity typically outweigh the risks. That may include anything from a spontaneous joke or story that has not been "field tested" all the way up to inviting audience members onstage for an impromptu interview.

Here's another reality: Sometimes spontaneous moments come whether you want them to or not! We've already mentioned several times that technology can be especially glitchy. Or you might have an audience member who is a little more responsive—or even a little more inebriated—than decorum would allow. In such moments, your spontaneous and genuine reactions can guide the audience through what otherwise might have derailed the entire experience.

Spontaneity is also helpful when things aren't going well. If there's a disconnect between yourself and your audience, sometimes the answer is not to keep plowing ahead and hope everything gets better. Instead, being willing to throw caution to the wind and try something new can create the connectivity you seek.

Activity: Do something spontaneous right now by calling someone on the phone you have not talked to in a long while. Don't give any reasons for your call; just dial the number and give yourself to the chat.

1) What emotions did you experience at the beginning of that conversation?

_____

_____

_____

_____

2) In general, how comfortable do you feel with spontaneous or unplanned moments as a communicator? Explain.

_____

_____

_____

_____

3) Is there a way to improve at being spontaneous? Explain your answer.

_____

_____

_____

_____

Speaking of spontaneity, you will encounter moments as a communicator when something "other" invades the connection between yourself and your audience. For example, I've spoken at many venues where the thermostat must have been stuck on "Arctic." I could see people shivering in their seats and trying to wrap up in whatever was available. As a communicator, I could choose to ignore that reality and simply plow through my planned presentation. But I've found the better response is to acknowledge what's happening and seek to find a solution. "It feels cold in here—could we turn up the heat a bit?" Even if no solution is forthcoming, simply acknowledging what your audience is experiencing can make the situation more endurable for all involved.

Many times these "elephant in the room" experiences can be much more serious. If you have been booked as a speaker at an event for months, but there is a tragedy that occurs either locally or nationally the night before your presentation, you are again faced with a choice. Will you conduct business as usual? Or will you express the truth of what has happened and actively validate what your audience is feeling in that moment?

Ignoring those elephants will often hamper your ability to connect with your hearers. In fact, you may all be in danger of being trampled by them! I recommend you choose to accept the responsibility your microphone has imposed on you and do your best to lead everyone involved to a better place.

1) When have you experienced one of these "elephant in the room" moments as a communicator?

_____

_____

_____

_____

2) Is it possible to prepare for such moments? Explain.

_____

_____

_____

_____

Another way your mic can become "hot" is when you are planning to share a message that you know many in the audience will have difficulty receiving. That can include teaching something that is challenging or controversial, relaying bad news or a difficult decision, confronting an issue that needs to be addressed, and so on.

Talk about pressure!

The best communicators typically approach such opportunities with gentleness and respect. Yes, you may have a difficult job to do. And yes, there may be people in the audience who need a kick in the pants or a wake-up call of some kind. Yet there is a way to accomplish those tasks without causing unnecessary harm or distress to those who hear you. As the one with the mic, it's your responsibility to find that way.

Please note that such moments are not limited to in-person events. Technology has vastly expanded our ability to communicate—which means technology has vastly expanded our ability to be harmful in our communication. You will need to choose whether to lean into the anonymity of such opportunities and take a "rip off the Band-Aid approach," or to communicate in a way that elevates the intrinsic value of those who hear you.

1) Do you relish or abhor opportunities to demonstrate "tough love." Explain.

_____

_____

_____

_____

2) What are some practical ways to respect others even when you need to deliver bad news?

_____

_____

_____

_____

3) How has technology expanded your ability to communicate?

_____

_____

_____

_____

CHAPTER 13

The Recipe

A note from Bishop Jakes:

As I shared with you at the beginning of this study, my conversations with Dr. Frank Thomas served as the catalyst for my resources on this topic of communication. The more he and I discussed their creation, the more I realized that maximum impact would be achieved with the rhetorical analysis only Frank could provide. If I considered my preaching to be like my grandmother's cooking without a recipe, then Dr. Thomas was not only determined to record my recipes but also to season them with his insight, acumen, and vast historical knowledge.

That's what we seek to accomplish in the final three chapters of the book. Since Dr. Thomas wrote these chapters, he will be your guide for them.

Because of my vocation as a pastor and Dr. Thomas's particular expertise in the art of sermon crafting, the immediate focus of the material will be on preaching. However, I am confident that communicators of any stripe and method will be inspired and encouraged by Dr. Thomas's words and insights.

Bon appétit!

I don't know how your grandmother cooks, but it has been my experience that many grandmas of my generation have a style and flair in the kitchen that are all their own. With decades of experience, they know how to create luscious foods and delectable desserts with a combination of instinct and expertise that is a joy to watch.

For this reason, many such grandmas forgo the use of recipes. They know how to do what they do without writing down instructions and measurements and the like.

But what about when Grandma is not available? If you don't have the opportunity to observe her and mimic her methods, what hope do you have of re-creating her best-loved dishes? Very little, to be sure. Therefore, there is value in recording recipes for posterity.

In a similar way, Bishop Jakes has been a top-notch communicator for decades, especially in the medium of preaching. He has not followed prescriptive recipes in crafting his messages; rather, he has "cooked" his sermons the same way Grandma delivers desserts.

What I hope to do in the final chapters of this study guide is help you gain a greater understanding of Bishop's recipe as a communicator. Not to reduce what he does to mere measurements, but to quantify his instincts in a way that enhances your own.

1) Where do you see similarities between crafting a message for communication and preparing a meal?

_____

_____

_____

2) Where do you see differences?

_____

_____

_____

_____

3) To what degree have you developed a "recipe" in your own efforts as a communicator?

_____

_____

_____

_____

One critical element of Bishop Jakes's "recipe" as a communicator is the African American tradition of orators that went before him. I firmly believe that no preacher is greater than the tradition from which they were birthed, simply because that tradition plays such a vital role in inspiring us, developing us, and releasing us to make our own contributions.

Not surprisingly, Bishop Jakes has benefited immensely from what Zora Neale Hurston described as the "characteristics of Negro expression," and those characteristics are vividly evident within his preaching.

For example, drama is a vital aspect of the African American tradition in general, which includes the preaching tradition specifically. There is little that is boring or mundane about African American worship and preaching. Instead, there are dramatic displays of exuberance. Both preaching and worship are interactive, built on a foundation of call and response. And African American preachers have traditionally displayed great freedom of expression, body movement, vocal performance, body language, and humor.

In short, for Bishop Jakes and other African American preachers, the act of preaching itself is dramatic cultural performance.

1) What have you appreciated most from your experiences with African American preaching, including that of Bishop Jakes?

_____

_____

_____

_____

2) How do you seek to incorporate drama and performance into your efforts at communication?

_____

_____

_____

_____

Zora Neale Hurston described two additional elements of the African American experience that are evident within black preaching. The first is "the will to adorn." Hurston described the way many Negro houses were bursting with decorations and displays of all kinds—jewelry, artistic expressions, sculptures, fabrics, and more. For black families, the desire to find and indulge in beauty has long been foundational.

The same is true for black preachers. They decorate, adorn, and embroider words and narration with the figurative language of metaphor and simile with the intent to satisfy "the desire for beauty" in the congregation's and preacher's souls. Bishop Jakes has said that the preacher must have enough substance to justify their style, not merely imitating others but adding their own descriptive, decorative flair.

The preacher—in language dripping with picturesque imagery, poetry, hyperbole, and alliteration, all based on the five senses of the audience—creates beauty for themselves and their audience. The sermon is adorned to create beauty in the human soul. Without question, the African American preacher is a master of adornment.

Activity: Take a few moments to skim back over the contents of this study guide, along with the book. Read over some of the passages you have enjoyed most.

1) Where do you see evidence of Bishop Jakes's appreciation for beauty and adornment as a communicator?

_____

_____

_____

_____

2) What can you tell about Bishop Jakes's appreciation of language and imagery?

_____

_____

_____

_____

The third characteristic of African American expression identified by Zora Neale Hurston is a reliance on folklore and storytelling. Indeed, storytelling is the overarching method of black expression, including black preaching. That has been true for centuries of our history, and it is true today.

What is storytelling? It's the ability to start with abstract truth and place it in the context of everyday life. It's the ability to speak the truth using characters, pictures, and stories. Black preachers in particular have learned that our audiences respond much better—and retain ideas more fully—when they are appealed to through story rather than abstract facts or doctrines.

1) How do you incorporate storytelling in your efforts at communication?

_____

_____

_____

_____

2) Where do you see storytelling having a prominent role in today's culture? What about black culture specifically?

_____

_____

_____

_____

One term that is often associated with black culture and black preachers is *soul*. There are lots of ways to describe or understand that term, but Bishop Jakes has long believed that the *soul* inherent in the African American experience is the ability to turn pain into power.

Of course, whether on continental Africa or within the many countries in which black folk currently reside, our history has been one of pain and strife. Apartheid and chattel slavery alone are some of the darkest stains visible in human history. As a result, the black experience is intrinsically wound up with the horror and terrible consequences of such institutions.

For the black preacher, then, there is a special pressure to help hearers make sense out of such a nonsensical history. Black preaching has a way of grounding itself in the grief and fear and moaning of the black experience, but then bringing order and structure to that pain so as to produce hope, victory, and vindication.

In many ways, this idea of *soul* goes beyond turning pain into power and has become a critical method for transmogrifying despair into hope.

1) How have you been shaped and refined as a communicator by the presence of pain?

_____

_____

_____

_____

2) What ideas or images come to mind when you hear the word *soul*?

_____

_____

_____

3) What would it look like for you to focus on turning despair into hope as a communicator?

_____

_____

_____

CHAPTER 14

The Ingredients

In addition to thinking through a recipe for Bishop Jakes's approach to preaching and communication, it's also helpful to identify some of the "ingredients" he uses most. First and foremost, like all preachers, it's clear that Bishop Jakes begins his "cooking" with a healthy appreciation for tradition.

By "tradition," I am speaking of the values, experiences, and beliefs of a specific community. The common language and collective memories. These are the raw materials from which preachers create their sermons. And it is through this lens of tradition that hearers process and engage with those sermons.

What I am describing is a symbiotic relationship. The preacher is steeped in the tradition of the community and receives his own training and development within the boundaries of that tradition. Then, through the act of creating and orating, the preacher adds his own unique expressions based on his own unique personality and experiences. Then, he offers his creation back to the community to reinvigorate the values, experiences, and beliefs of that tradition.

1) What are some of the core values and beliefs of the tradition in which you were raised?

_____

_____

_____

2) How do those core values and beliefs make their way into your communication, whether preaching or other forms?

_____

_____

_____

3) In what ways have you been able to reshape those values and beliefs with your own personality and experiences?

_____

_____

_____

As mentioned previously, storytelling is a key component of Bishop Jakes's preaching and overall communication. It is one of the raw ingredients he appreciates most and uses liberally.

As he should! Effective storytelling has been part of black preaching for as long as there has been such a thing as black preaching. Moreover, storytelling is key for connecting to audiences of all kinds.

In Bishop's case, his ability to both weave and appreciate stories came from his mother. She, too, was a storyteller, and her regular communication through that medium was what first awakened him to its power. In fact, Bishop's mother would often preside over family talent shows when the children were younger as a way of both passing time and entertaining everyone involved on a limited budget.

His ability to tell stories is now automatic within Bishop's mind, and so this talent automatically expresses itself through his preaching. Details, characters, settings and scenes, plot twists—all the essential ingredients of good storytelling are accessible without even requiring conscious thought.

Activity: Read the story below, which came from Bishop Jakes. When finished, answer the questions to unpack your experience.

I'm coming around the road from delivering papers, a mountain road in Charleston, West Virginia, and all these puppies were trying to nurse. They were newborn puppies and the German shepherd mother was dead. And they were trying to nurse at the breast of a dead mother.

I put all the puppies in a box and I brought them home. I guess I'm about seven or eight years old. I decided I was going to make them live. So I poured out Momma's Palmolive dishwashing liquid and put some warm milk in the bottle and a little bit of oatmeal and—I don't know why, don't ask me why—but that seemed like it would be good. And I put it in there and warmed it up a little bit and I nursed the puppies.

Well, two things I learned. First is if the right person picks you up and they fight hard enough, they make you live, because the puppies all lived. I didn't lose any of them. Second, I learned that oatmeal gives puppies diarrhea. Really bad diarrhea.

I think I'm still that little boy gathering up puppies. At my core I still am that guy who will pick you up where you're at and feed you whatever I got to get you up on your feet so you can fulfill your destiny. And that's my blessed hope.

1) What is your initial reaction to this story? Why?

_____

_____

_____

_____

2) What are some key elements or details that make it an effective story?

_____

_____

_____

3) What are specific ways you can incorporate these kinds of stories into your communication?

_____

_____

_____

_____

Two more raw ingredients that are well represented in Bishop Jakes's preaching are the Bible and hope. Of course, you would expect the Bible to be a primary ingredient for any preacher, and hopefully that is so. In Bishop's case, however, I am struck by his deep devotion for God's Word. Ever since he was a child, Bishop Jakes has found comfort and meaning and purpose within the pages of Scripture, and his devotion to those pages shows out through the respect and devotion he gives them in his preaching.

Bishop Jakes is also a deeply hopeful preacher. He is an optimist, and the root of his optimism is the fervent belief that God is with him in all that he does. Moreover, this optimism spills out and over the audience when Bishop preaches. He believes not only that God is with him, but also that God desires to be and will be present in the lives of any who reach out for him. Therefore, Bishop Jakes's sermons are inherently hope-filled.

1) How would you describe your connection to or relationship with the Bible?

_____

_____

_____

2) Why is Scripture an effective raw ingredient for many types of communication?

_____

_____

_____

_____

3) Where does the idea of hope fit within your current approach to communication?

_____

_____

_____

_____

Every good sermon has many ingredients in common, and one of the most important is what preachers often call "the close." That is the end of the sermon experience. This typically includes a summary of the sermon's overall message, in addition to some form of application—a challenge or inspiring call for hearers to live out the truth expressed in that message.

As you might expect, Bishop Jakes is a master of the close. Part of his effectiveness at ending a sermon has to do with the overall delivery of that sermon from beginning to end. This includes the raw ingredients of tradition, storytelling, Scripture, and hope, as described earlier. This also includes Bishop Jakes's tremendous energy and passion expressed through body language. Indeed, many have marveled at the way he can "play" his body and facial expressions and tone of voice the way experienced musicians play their instruments.

When it comes time to finish the sermon experience, then, his hearers have been elevated to heights of expectancy and appreciation. They are ready for the crux of the message and the call to obey what God has spoken through the preacher.

In my conversations with Bishop Jakes, he has made it clear there is no preferred "method" for the closing of a sermon. It is common in the black community for preacher and audience alike to join in standing and shouting as evidence of the Holy Spirit's presence. Yet Bishop believes the close of each sermon should be a unique and natural expression of what has already taken place through that sermon.

What is important is that hearers understand what they have experienced and how they have been changed by it.

1) How do you typically "close" your efforts at communication?

_____

_____

_____

_____

2) What do you hope your audience experiences during those final moments? Why?

_____

_____

_____

_____

CHAPTER 15

The Taste

The goal of cooking a meal is not the cooking itself. Rather, the goal is to be nourished by the final result. To indulge in the flavors of well-prepared food. To enjoy the company and family and friends around the table. To savor the delight of both culinary and conversational success.

In a similar way, we don't follow the "recipe" of preaching—or more broadly, of communication in general—simply to prepare a message. We indulge in the process of communication in order to communicate. To savor that moment of expressing ourselves so that we may both understand and be understood. This is true not only for preaching but for any form of communication. The recipe and the ingredients and the hard work all culminate in that moment when everyone gets to "taste" the final result.

For preachers, the Holy Spirit has a lot to do with the final "taste" of a sermon experience. The best preachers understand they are not engaging in the act of communication by themselves. Neither is the audience. Rather, as both preacher and hearers engage together around the truth of God's Word, the Holy Spirit uplifts the experience to the satisfaction of everyone involved.

Ultimately, the goal of a sermon experience—and the goal of many types of communication—is persuasion. The speaker is following his recipe and combining his ingredients in such a way as to lead the hearer in a new direction.

1) What do you enjoy most about the "taste" of communicating? Why?

_____

_____

_____

_____

2) How much of the end result of your communication is up to you, and how much of it relies on something "other"?

_____

_____

_____

_____

3) What does success look like for you as a communicator?

_____

_____

_____

_____

If persuasion is a key goal of the preaching experience, it makes sense to ask the question "Who are you trying to persuade?" As I have studied the sermons of Bishop Jakes, I have seen the way he takes a broad approach in presenting his material so that he appeals to a broader audience. Indeed, Bishop believes that broad thinking is necessary for galvanizing disparate groups of people.

For preachers specifically (and communicators in general), it is relatively easy to be persuasive when you are speaking with people who already think the way you think and believe what you believe. It's quite another experience to express your persuasive message to people who are not inclined to follow it. Thus, speaking to a broader audience is much more challenging than "preaching to the choir."

With this in mind, the breadth of Bishop's audience is truly impressive. In any given week, he preachers for an audience that includes homeless people off the streets and doctors fresh from their latest shifts. He calls together chemists, lawyers, plumbers, teachers, and hearers of every vocation. On a regular basis, he speaks to diverse America whether they are black, white, Latinx, Nigerian, Ghanaian, Barbadian, Bahamian, or Jamaican.

How can a communicator hold together such a wide array of participants? By taking a broad approach to both the message and the medium. By building bridges rather than seeking to tear down.

Activity: Spend some time listening to one of Bishop Jakes's sermons. "I Didn't Know I Was Me," which is referenced in the appendix of the book, is a good option.

1) Where do you see evidence in Bishop's sermon that he is speaking to a broad spectrum of people?

_____

_____

_____

_____

2) Where in Bishop's sermon did you hear examples of seeking to build bridges and unify people?

_____

_____

_____

_____

3) What are some bigger ideas that are galvanizing people in today's world?

_____

_____

_____

_____

I have made the effort in these final chapters to explain the recipe and the ingredients of effective orators such as Bishop Jakes. Yet there is another aspect that is important in achieving success as a communicator. That aspect is desire, or what we might often refer to as "drive."

In the words of Bishop Jakes, if you want to excel at preaching or any other expression of communication, you have to want it. You have to want to be successful with the same passion and desperate desire as a drowning man wants to push above the waves and pull in just one more gasp of sweet-tasting air.

Unfortunately, most communicators lack that desire. Preachers especially can develop an attitude of, "It will happen if God wants it to happen." Almost a fatalism. To speak frankly, such an attitude simply won't cut it. To be great at anything requires great effort. Titanic desire. It requires working through the night when others go to bed. It requires rising up and refusing to quit even when challenges seem insurmountable. And it requires a willingness to be dogged and single-focused in a world that is constantly trying to distract our attention with shiny objects and fleeting pleasures.

1) Using the scale below, how would you rate your level of drive or "want to" when it comes to excelling as a communicator?

1	2	3	4	5	6	7	8	9	10

(No drive)   (I want it!)

2) What obstacles are currently holding you back from rising higher in your field of communication?

_____

_____

_____

_____

3) What steps will you need to take to overcome these obstacles, and why haven't you taken them?

_____

_____

_____

Let us conclude this exploration of Bishop's recipe for communication success by looking once more at some of the keys to his success. First, remember that Bishop's sermon-preparation process includes four steps: Study yourself full, think yourself clear, pray yourself hot, and let yourself go. As Bishop Jakes mentioned earlier, it's likely a bad idea for you to copy this process step for step. Yet it is important for you to *have* a process. Specifically, you need to have a method that allows you to evaluate your effectiveness each time you put it into practice.

In addition, Bishop Jakes has continually reminded me that when a preacher (or any communicator) mounts the stage, everything about that person is communicating. The question to ask is: *Does my mouth out-communicate the rest of me?* Are you speaking effectively through your gestures? The timbre of your voice? Are you communicating with your hearers or simply talking at them? All of these are key considerations for preachers and communicators alike.

Finally, remember that the art of communication reflects the recipes inherited, the ingredients chosen, the process of blending and cooking—all in order to serve messages as soul food with exquisite flavor. If you wish to create cravings in those who hear you speak (or read what you write) so that they savor each of your offerings, then you cannot overlook any part of the process. No matter how much work went into the preparation and process, ultimately, the taste is what will be remembered.

1) What have you appreciated most about this study? Why?

_____

_____

_____

_____

2) What specific actions or takeaways will you use to improve your communication?

_____

_____

_____

3) Where do you have opportunities right now to continue building experience and growing as a communicator?

_____

_____

_____